D0064837

# Careers without College

# Retail
# Salesperson

## by *Charnan Simon*

**Content Consultant**:
Jenney Radcliffe
Manager, Internal Communications
Target Stores

C A P S T O N E
H I G H / L O W  B O O K S
an imprint of Capstone Press

# C A P S T O N E     P R E S S

## 818 North Willow Street • Mankato, Minnesota 56001

http://www.capstone-press.com

*Library of Congress Cataloging-in-Publication Data*
Simon, Charnan.
    Retail salesperson / by Charnan Simon.
      p.cm. -- (Careers without college)
    Includes bibliographical references and index.
    Summary: Outlines the educational requirements, duties, salary, employment outlook, and possible future positions for retail sales personnel.
    ISBN 1-56065-708-1
    1. Selling--Vocational guidance--United States--Juvenile literature. 2. Retail trade--Vocational guidance--United States--Juvenile literature. 3. Sales personnel--United States--Juvenile literature. [1. Retail trade--Vocational guidance. 2. Sales personnel. 3. Vocational guidance.]
I. Title. II. Series: Careers without college (Mankato, Minn.)
HF5439.5.S55 1998
381'.1'02373--DC21
                         97-40910
                           CIP
                           AC

**Photo Credits:**
International Stock/Mark Bolster, 14; Jeff Greenberg, 17
Photo Network/Tom Tracy, 12
James L. Shaffer, 4, 18, 25, 30, 34
Unicorn Stock Photos/Deneve Feigh Bunde, 6; Jeff Greenberg, cover, 22, 32, 39;
   Dennis MacDonald, 11; Tom McCarthy, 36
Valan Photos/Kennon Cooke, 29; Richard T. Nowitz, 9, 21, 41, 44; Harold
   Rosenberg, 26

# Table of Contents

# Fast Facts

Career Title _____ Retail Salesperson

Minimum Educational
Requirement _____ High school diploma

Certification Requirement _____ Nonc

U.S. Salary Range _____ $8,840 to $31,800

Canadian Salary Range_____ $10,700 to $51,000
(Canadian dollars)

U.S. Job Outlook _____ About as fast as average

Canadian Job Outlook _____ Much faster than the average

DOT Cluster_____ Clerical and Sales Occupations
(Dictionary of Occupational Titles)

DOT Number _____ 290.477-014

GOE Number_____ 09.04.02
(Guide for Occupational Exploration)

NOC _____ 6421
(National Occupational Classification—Canada)

# Chapter 1

# Job Responsibilities

Retail salespeople help customers find and buy goods in stores. A customer is someone who buys items from a store. Retail salespeople sell many kinds of goods and services. They work in big cities and small towns. They work in small stores and large department stores.

Retail salespeople must be friendly. They must be able to talk about the items they sell. Many

**Retail salespeople sell many kinds of goods and services.**

retail salespeople also handle money and must be good with numbers.

## On the Job

A retail salesperson's most important duty is to help customers find what they want. Retail salespeople must know about the products they sell. They must be able to explain how one item differs from another. They must try to answer all their customers' questions.

Good retail salespeople pay attention to customers' needs. Retail salespeople greet customers as they enter stores or departments. Some customers like to browse. Browse means to look at an item to consider buying it. Some customers may be looking for a specific item. They need help right away.

Many retail salespeople also enter sales in cash registers. They must know how to handle cash, checks, and charge cards. Sometimes retail salespeople gift wrap purchases. They might

**A retail salesperson's most important duty is to help customers find what they want.**

arrange for items to be sent to customers' homes. They also take back items that customers decide they do not want.

## Other Duties

Sometimes stores do not have the items customers want. Retail salespeople may try to order the items or find them at another store. Retail salespeople also might suggest another item for the customer to buy.

Retail salespeople stay busy even when there are no customers in stores. They straighten and clean their work areas. They set up new displays and mark price tags. They learn about items that are on sale. Retail salespeople may count money. They may also put the money in store safes or banks.

**Retail salespeople sometimes set up new displays.**

# Chapter 2

# What the Job Is Like

Retail salespeople can work many different hours. Some work during the day. Others work at night. Many also work weekends and holidays. Companies look for retail salespeople who are friendly and polite. These workers help bring more customers to stores.

**Many retail salespeople work part time.**

## Hours

Retail salespeoples' hours may change often. Sometimes they work only in the mornings. Sometimes retail salespeople work weekends or at night. Full-time workers work 40 hours per week.

Many retail salespeople work part time. Part-time workers work less than 40 hours per week. This can be helpful for workers who have responsibilities at home or at school. Retail salespeople do not always choose which hours they work.

Many stores are busy on weekends and during the holidays. Retail salespeople work many hours at these times. They might even work on holidays.

## Work Setting

Most stores are comfortable places to work. But retail sales work can be challenging. Salespeople

**Retail salespeople stand much of the time.**

stand much of the time. But they receive breaks during the day.

Most workers wear their own clothes to work. But some stores have dress codes. Some retail salespeople must wear uniforms that stores supply. Stores may give their retail salespeople special aprons or jackets to wear.

## Personal traits

Good retail salespeople have certain personal traits. They are friendly. They must like working with the public. Retail salespeople must get along with many kinds of people. They need to be polite to all customers.

Good retail salespeople are self-starters. They find ways to stay busy during slow periods. They are not bothered easily. They stay calm when stores are busy.

**A good retail salesperson must be friendly and knowledgeable.**

# Chapter 3

# Training

Stores look for certain skills in the people they hire for retail sales positions. English, speech, and math are good courses to take in preparation for retail sales work. Retail salespeople must be able to speak well. They must understand customers' needs. They also need to be able to add, subtract, multiply, and divide correctly.

**Retail salespeople must have good math skills.**

## Advanced Skills

Some retail salespeople need more advanced skills. For example, retail salespeople who sell computers should understand how computers work. Retail salespeople who sell car parts should understand how cars work.

The most successful retail salespeople sell products they know and like. They are able to help answer customers' questions.

## Training Programs

Many junior or community colleges have special training programs for retail salespeople. Students learn about running retail stores. Students learn how to sell different items. They also learn how to work with customers. Students learn about how stores plan for sales. They also learn about advertising.

Some schools offer on-the-job training programs to students. Students earn grades

**The most successful retail salespeople sell products they know and like.**

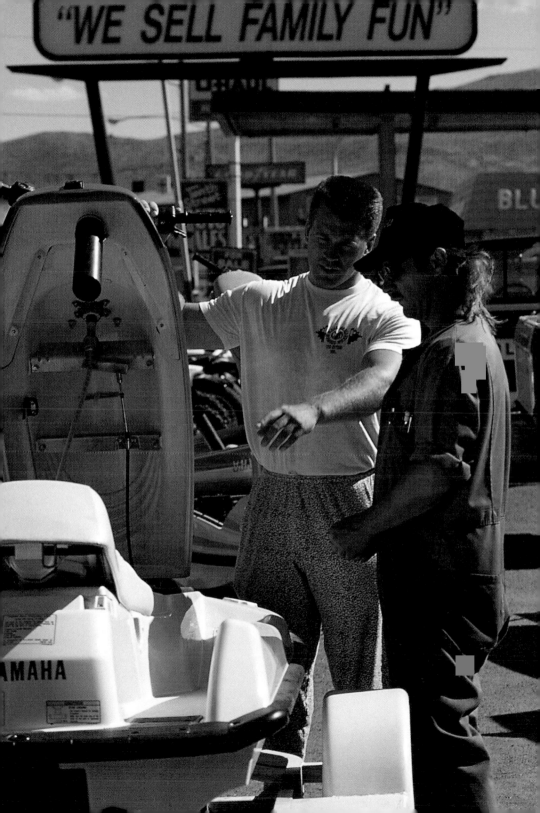

and money at the same time. Many students become full-time retail salespeople when they finish these programs.

## On-the-Job Training

Most stores offer some kind of in-store training. In small stores, owners or managers may train new employees. A manager is a person who is in charge of a department or an entire store. Most large stores offer more formal training programs. These programs usually last two or three days. Salespeople receive their regular wages while they are in training.

Retail salespeople learn how to greet customers. They learn how to display goods in their departments. Retail salespeople also learn how to keep track of products. They learn how to tell customers about the products they are selling.

**In small stores, owners or managers may train new employees.**

Retail salespeople learn how to run cash registers. Most cash registers are computers. New workers spend time learning how to operate these machines.

Retail salespeople learn about store rules in their training programs. They learn about any special dress codes stores might have. They also learn where and when to take breaks.

**Retail salespeople learn how to tell customers about the products they are selling.**

# Chapter 4

# Salary and Job Outlook

Wages for retail salespeople vary greatly. Many new retail salespeople earn the federal minimum wage. Some earn more. Minimum wage is the lowest amount a company can pay a worker.

## Salary

Stores pay most retail salespeople by the hour. Large stores usually offer starting wages higher

**Stores pay most retail salespeople by the hour.**

27

than the minimum wage. Retail salespeople might also earn more if there are not enough people to fill a store's positions. A shortage of workers encourages employers to pay workers more money to keep them.

Experienced workers earn more than those who are just learning. Workers with special job skills or knowledge also earn more money.

In the United States, full-time retail salespeople earn an average of $18,096 per year. Most retail salespeople earn between $10,800 and $22,440 per year. Some workers earn more than $31,800 per year.

In Canada, full-time retail salespeople earn an average of $28,900 per year. One in ten workers earns more than $51,000 per year.

## Commission

Many retail salespeople earn commissions in addition to their wages. A commission is a part of the total sales a retail salesperson makes. Some

**Experienced retail salespeople earn more than those who are just starting out.**

neg. pages
XSE
Mcar

the total sales a retail salesperson makes. Some retail salespeople work entirely on commission.

Retail salespeople can increase their earnings by working on commission. They earn more money if they sell more goods. But working on commission also has problems. Even the best retail salesperson can have weeks with few sales. Regular wages are more dependable.

Workers who sell costly items such as cars, furniture, and electronics usually work on commission. These retail salespeople can make the most money if they sell many items. They must have experience and knowledge.

## Benefits
Most retail salespeople can buy their stores' products at discounted prices. A discounted price is less than the full price. Discounted prices usually range from 10 percent to 25 percent off the regular price.

**Retail salespeople who sell costly items such as electronics usually earn commissions.**

Most large stores offer their full-time retail salespeople health insurance. Health insurance is protection from the costs of getting sick. People pay a small amount to insurance companies each month. The insurance companies will pay most of the bills if a person becomes sick.

Some stores also give pensions. Pensions are payments to older people who have retired. Large stores also may offer paid vacation and sick leave. They might have dinners or give awards to top sellers. Small stores often cannot provide these benefits. At this time, part-time workers may not receive benefits.

## Job Outlook

The number of retail stores is growing. Customers buy items from stores every day. Store owners hire salespeople to meet their customers' needs. There will always be a strong demand for retail salespeople. Because of this, retail salespeople can count on having steady jobs.

**Most large stores offer benefits to their full-time retail salespeople.**

# Chapter 5

# Where the Job Can Lead

Retail salespeople have many job opportunities. Most stores hire extra part-time workers during busy holiday seasons. Students and new retail salespeople often work part time.

Retail sales work varies from store to store. Retail salespeople may open stores in the morning. They set up displays and place

**Retail salespeople perform a variety of tasks.**

special orders. They count inventory and unpack goods. A good retail salesperson with energy and a good attitude often can move up to a supervisor position quickly. Supervisors oversee the work of other workers.

Retail salespeople in large stores usually develop specialized skills. They become good at selling one type of item, such as furniture or men's clothing. They can become senior retail salespeople or supervisors. They might advance to a manager position.

## Manager Programs

Some large stores offer manager training programs. These programs train people to become store managers. Stores usually look for college graduates for these programs. Some well-trained and smart retail salespeople also enter the programs.

**Retail salespeople can become supervisors.**

Retail salespeople also move into other areas of retail sales. They can become buyers. Buyers decide what goods to sell in departments or stores. Retail salespeople with good math skills might move into accounting departments. Retail salespeople with artistic skills can move into advertising. Workers who write and speak well might move into public relations. Public relations is showing a good image to the community.

## A Future in Retail Sales

Retail sales is the second-largest business in the United States. There are nearly two million retail stores in the country. Almost five million retail salespeople work in these stores.

Customers look for good products in stores. They look for low prices. Stores

**Buyers decide what goods to sell in departments or stores.**

look for friendly retail salespeople to help customers find what they want.

Customers spend millions of dollars in retail stores every day. New stores open all the time. These stores need retail sales workers to help sell their products. Retail salespeople have many job opportunities.

**Customers look for good products in stores.**

# Words to Know

**browse** (BROUZ)—to look at an item to consider buying it

**commission** (kuh-MISH-uhn)—the part of the total sales a retail salesperson makes

**customer** (KUHSS-tuh-mur)—someone who buys items in a store

**health insurance** (HELTH in-SHU-ruhnss)—protection from the costs of getting sick

**manager** (MAN-uh-jur)—a person who is in charge of a department or an entire store

**minimum wage** (MIN-uh-muhm WAJE)—the lowest amount a company can pay a worker

**pension** (PEN-shuhn)—payments to older people who have retired

**supervisor** (SOO-pur-vye-zur)—a person who oversees the work of others

# To Learn More

**Brescoll, James and Ralph M. Dahm**. *Opportunities in Sales Careers*. Lincolnwood, Ill.: VGM Career Horizons, 1995.

**Brown, Ronald**. *From Selling to Managing: Guidelines for the First-Time Sales Manager*. New York: American Management Association, 1990.

**Epstein, Lawrence S**. *Careers in Computer Sales*. New York: Rosen Pub. Group, 1990.

**Frisch, Carlienne**. *Careers Inside the World of Sales*. New York: Rosen Pub. Group, 1995.

# Useful Addresses

**National Retail Federation**
325 Seventh Street, NW
Washington, D.C. 20004-2802

**National Retail Merchant Association**
100 West 31st Street
New York, NY 10001

**North American Retail Dealers Association**
10 East 22nd Street
Suite 310
Lombard, IL 60148

# Internet Sites

**National Retail Federation**
http://www.nrf.com

**National Retail Institute**
http://www.nrf.com/nri/nri.htm

**Retail**
http://www.youthworks.ca/yw20.htm

**Retail Sales Workers**
http://stats.bls.gov/oco/ocos121.htm

# Index